Lutz Heusinger
Fabrizio Mancinelli

The Sistine Chapel

Scala Books
distributed by Harper & Row, Publishers

CONTENTS

LIST OF ILLUSTRATIONS FOLLOWING THE TEXT

* * * * * * * * * * *

SCALA, Istituto Fotografico Editoriale, Firenze
Editors: Francesco Papafava, Barbara Gökgöl
Translation: Rowena Fajardo
Layout: Fried Rosenstock
Photographs: SCALA, except: p. 7, Alinari; pp. 11, 13, 17, 23, 25, 31, British Museum, London; p. 11, Detroit Institute of Arts; p. 26, Buonarroti Archive, Florence; p. 29, Uffizi, Florence

Printed in Italy by Officine Grafiche Firenze 1984

Fabrizio Mancinelli

I. The Sistine Chapel

Built in the time of Pope Sixtus IV della Rovere (1471-1484), from whom it takes its name, the Sistine Chapel had originally the functions both of Palatine Chapel and of keep for the complex of buildings set in a square around the Court of the " Pappagallo ", the most ancient center of the Apostolic palaces. Later on, as times changed and the Belvedere Courtyard, Borgia Courtyard and Courts of the Sentinel and of St. Damasus came into being, giving a Renaissance character to the papal residence, it lost its defensive function, though the appearance remained, in the severe and massive structure of the exterior and the crenellation of the upper part.

It rises on the site of a " cappella magna " built in the palace by Nicholas III (1277-1280) and used as the popes' chapel up till 28th May 1473. The thirteenth-century chapel was destroyed, possibly because in a very poor state of repair, and the new building was begun according to the most reliable theory in 1475, the year of the Jubilee, when many other ecclesiastical buildings in Rome were erected.

The building comprises, vertically, a cellar, a mezzanine floor and the chapel, above which lies a spacious attic. The mezzanine floor, like the cellar, is divided into nine rooms, which were the offices of the " Magistri Ceremoniarum ". The outside walls rise smoothly, with their bricks visible, their expanse hardly interrupted by the openings that light the interior or by the slightly projecting cornices. They were crowned by crenellations supported by corbels, with a hole every two for throwing burning oil and other ammunition on possible attackers.

The chapel is very simple in shape; without an apse, it measures 40.93 meters long by 13.41 meters wide, that is, the dimensions that the Bible gives for the Temple of Solomon. It is 20.70 meters high, and roofed by a flattened barrel vault, with little side vaults over the centered windows. The smoothness of the walls, so designed for the pictorial decoration, is scarcely broken into, as PAGE 33 on the outside, by three cornices, of which the middle and widest one forms a gallery running right round the chapel at the level of the windows. A low marble seat runs along the walls on three sides in the area reserved for the faithful. The floor is of colored marble inlay, showing how the tradition of the Roman marble workers was still alive in the late fifteenth century, and highlights by the differences in its geometrical patterns the areas into which the space of the church was divided (distinguished also by differences in level and by the screen). On one side is the presbytery, with the altar and the pope's throne, reserved for officiating clergy, and on the other the space for the faithful. The marble screen with trellises, a free rendering of the Byzantine iconostasis, was moved back during the reign of Gregory XIII to enlarge the presbytery, but originally was attached to the " cantoria " which, as in Florentine churches, replaces the " schola cantorum ". Both are decorated with very delicate reliefs, the work of Mino da Fiesole, possibly assisted by Andrea Bregno and Giovanni Dalmata.

According to Vasari, the architect called to construct the new building was the Florentine Baccio Pontelli, to whom the pope probably entrusted also the construction of the Della Rovere palace in Borgo Vecchio; the documents, however, mention only Giovannino de' Dolci, who is called " superstans sive commissarius fabrice palacii apostolici ". It is probable, in view of his absence from Rome during those years, that Baccio Pontelli made the plans, and they were then carried out by Giovannino de' Dolci, who also supervised the decoration. In 1477 the building was well advanced, and in 1480 it must already have been finished, because in 1481 Perugino, Botticelli, Ghirlandaio and Cosimo Rosselli signed a contract to paint ten " stories " in the Sistine Chapel and in the document specific reference is made to frescoes already done.

The arrangement of the chapel, its size and the iconographical programme of the decoration show that the intention of Sixtus IV was to translate into Renaissance terms the composition and structure of the great Paleo-Christian and Medieval basilicas of which there were so many living reminders in Rome.

II. The Original Decoration of the Chapel

The present decoration of the Sistine Chapel is very different from what was originally planned. The intervention of Michelangelo altered profoundly its severe fifteenth-century spatial quality, by bringing into it a whole world of images which overlay its architectural structures, almost replacing them, giving a highly dramatic character to the interior and introducing quite new illusionistic formal elements. When in 1483 the chapel was consecrated, Pier Matteo d'Amelia had painted the ceiling simply as a sky with stars, which centered attention on the decoration below and emphasized the strictly geometrical structure of the vault itself with its horizontal and vertical lines. The original iconographic plan for the decoration included on the wall behind the altar a great frescoed " altar-piece " with the *Assumption of the Virgin* and the two frescoes with the *Nativity* and the *Finding of Moses* which began the two cycles to continue along the side walls and terminate on the entrance wall. Above began the " gallery " of popes, while on the dado, in accordance with early Christian tradition, were painted simulated curtains. The frescoes on this wall were destroyed to make room for Michelangelo's *Last Judgment*, while the collapse of the architrave over the main door damaged irreparably those on the entrance wall (they were entirely repainted in 1560). Thus, of the original frescoes there remain only those on the side walls.

The decoration of the chapel was done in an incredibly short time, thanks to the close collaboration between the artists and their respective workshops, an example of teamwork rare in the painting of any age. The ambiguity of the documents, of which there are two, dated respectively 26th October 1481 and 17th January 1482, has given rise to contradictory hypotheses as to the chronology of the works. The most reliable, however, seems to be the following. First of all, perhaps in 1480, Perugino was called and decorated the wall behind the altar; later Botticelli, Ghirlandaio and Cosimo Rosselli arrived, and together with Perugino painted on the side wall the first four panels of the Christ cycle, with the curtains below and the corresponding portraits of popes. In October 1481 these four artists promised to carry out by March of the following year the ten remaining frescoes, with the curtains below them, and complete the series of the popes, on pain of forfeiting fifty ducats if they had not finished their work by the date set. Giovannino de' Dolci, of whom we have already spoken in regard to the construction of the chapel, was appointed supervisor of their work, although it is not clear to what extent he performed this task. Payment was to be calculated on the basis of the decoration already done on the side wall, which in January 1482 was estimated at two hundred and fifty gold ducats.

The four artists, helped by the workshops – which counted among their members Pinturicchio, Piero di Cosimo and Bartolomeo della Gatta – painted at the same time the scenes of the two cycles, Christ and Moses, and advanced parallel, as was the custom, toward the entrance wall. There must have been a preliminary agreement, as all the figures are uniform in size and the horizon line is at the same height in all the frescoes. The homogeneity of the whole, transcending the stylistic differences between the artists, has suggested that one particular artist may have been responsible for directing the others; Vasari maintains that Sixtus IV called Botticelli from Florence for this purpose, but it is more probable, if the theory is in fact true, that the part fell to Perugino; he was highly esteemed by his colleagues and since he had begun first the pattern of his works conditioned that of the others. It was he who painted the greatest number of scenes – besides those on the altar wall, he painted the *Baptism of Christ*, the *Handing over of the Keys to St. Peter* and the *Circumcision of the Son of Moses*. As for the others, Botticelli painted three panels, Ghirlandaio two and Cosimo Rosselli four. There has been some controversy over the attribution of the single scenes, but the account of Vasari, which is supported by stylistic indications, is generally accepted. The question of the portraits of the popes is more debatable, but in view of the terms of the contract it is probable that each artist was responsible for those above the scenes he himself painted. For reasons unknown to us, the decoration of the chapel was not finished by

Sistine Chapel
Reconstruction
of interior
before Julius II

the artists that began it, and in Autumn 1482 Luca Signorelli was commissioned to paint the two missing frescoes, the *Testament of the Moses* and the *Fight over the Body of Moses*. The next year the Chapel was completed, and on 15th August Sixtus IV della Rovere performed the solemn consecration, dedicating it to the Virgin of the Assumption (perhaps the name also of the thirteenth-century church).

The Stories of Moses originally began with the description of the early childhood of the prophet, and among the episodes in the lost fresco, according to Vasari, were the Birth and the Finding of Moses. The biblical account now begins with the *Journey of Moses*; in this panel, against a hilly background PAGE 34 we see in the fore the meeting of the Prophet and the Angel, sent by the Lord to punish him for his disobedience to the order to circumcise all his male children, and on the right the circumcision of his son. The title *Observatio antiquae regenerationis a Moise per circoncisionem* refers to this last episode, and in both scenes the figure of Zipporah, who becomes the main protagonist and who personifies the Church of Gentiles, is given great importance. In the background we see Moses taking leave of his father-in-law Jethro, before setting out on the journey back to Egypt during which he meets the Angel. The fresco is generally attributed to Perugino, who however was to an important extent assisted by Pinturicchio, probably the painter of the delicate landscape.

The second panel is the work of Botticelli, and illustrates as many as seven PAGE 35 events from the life of Moses. The story begins, below right, with the killing of the Egyptian who had maltreated a Jew (right) and the consequent flight into the desert (above). In the center is the meeting with the daughters of Jethro, whom Moses helps to water their flocks after chasing off (in the background) the shepherds who were trying to stop them. The most important episode, as regards iconographical content, is, however, that of the burning bush (above left) to which the title accompanying the painting refers (*Temptatio Moisi legis scriptae latoris*). This is a clear allusion to the test to which Yahweh subjected the prophet, ordering him to walk into the burning bush after taking off his shoes. The story finishes below with Israel leaving Egypt, led by Moses, who has become the guide and leader of his people.

The third panel, rather weak in composition, is generally attributed to Cosimo Rosselli and Piero di Cosimo, although it has also been suggested that it is by Ghirlandaio, who painted the *Calling of the First Apostles* opposite. It shows the *Crossing of the Red Sea*, and this single episode, in contrast to the previous PAGE 36 frescoes, takes up almost all the available space; the group of little figures in the background on the right probably represents Moses and Aaron before Pharaoh, who is granting them permission to leave Egypt.

The title *Congregatio populi a Moise scriptam accepturi* refers to the episode where the people are gathering joyfully around the figure of the Prophet (below left), for the first time singled out by the composition. Beyond the historical meaning, which can clearly be read in the scene, the inscription highlights a symbolic content, the expectation of the Law, and stresses the fact that this scene is a PAGE 36

prelude to the next in which the "promulgatio" of the Law takes place – the *Handing over of the Tables of the Law*. This painting also is by Cosimo Rosselli, and it is both the most archaizing and the weakest by the Florentine master. It seems that he had won the liking of the Pope who, as Vasari recounts, "did not understand much about these things, although he took great delight in them". This fresco, besides the Handing over the Tables of the Law (center above), comprises the Adoration of the Golden Calf (center background), Moses breaking the Tables of the Law (center foreground), the Punishment of the Idolaters (right above) and the return of Moses with the new Tables of the Law (left), to which more specifically the title *Promulgatio legis scriptae a Moise* refers. With this series of episodes the role of the prophet changes; from now on he is represented as a law-giver, and thus mediator between the Jews and God. Beside him Joshua is constantly seen, while the figure of Aaron is given slight importance.

The fifth panel, the most important of the series from the point of view of symbolic content, was painted by Botticelli, who presented a subject iconographically very rare, the *Punishment of Corah, Datan and Abiron*. In contrast PAGE 37 to the previous ones, the episodes are set in a landscape which we could call urban, dominated by three classical buildings of which two are clearly recognizable, the Septizonium on the right and in the center the arch of Constantine, the writing on which admonishes *Nemo sibi assum / at honorem nisi / vocatus a Deo / tamquam Aaron.* The action occurs in the foreground: on the right the attempt to stone Moses, referred to in the title (*Conturbatio Moisi legis scriptae latoris*); in the center, at a sign from Moses, the followers of Corah who were offering incense are consumed by an invisible fire, contrasting with Aaron, a hieratic priestly figure with a tiara; to the left, again at a sign from Moses, the earth opens up to swallow the blasphemers, while their children watch the scene in terror as if suspended on a cloud.

The last fresco on this wall is devoted to the *Testament of Moses* and was painted PAGE 37 by Luca Signorelli; lost, as we have already said, is the *Fight over the Body of Moses*, which concluded the series and was also by Signorelli. The present painting was entirely redone in 1560 by Matteo da Lecce, a mediocre Mannerist. The *Testament of Moses* is divided into five episodes set in a hilly landscape not very different in composition from that in the first fresco. The title *Replicatio legis scriptae a Moise* refers to the episode in the right foreground, showing the prophet as he reads the laws; in the center is the nude figure of the foreigner, and on the left Moses hands over the rod of command to Joshua. These two episodes stress the last aspect of the character of Moses, his priestly quality. In the background the angel shows Moses Jerusalem from the top of Mt. Horeb, while below he descends toward the place of his death, represented in the episode PAGE 39 on the left.

The Stories of Christ are also without the first scene representing the *Nativity*, which was destroyed to make place for Michelangelo's *Last Judgment*. The story now begins with the *Baptism of Christ*, the work of Perugino, whose signature PAGE 40 can be seen on the band above the scene. The Umbrian master was, however, largely assisted by Pinturicchio, who probably painted most of the figures, excepting the central group, and the delicate landscape in the background. The Baptism which occupies the center foreground of the panel is referred to in the title, *Institutio novae regenerationis a Christo in Baptismo*, which stresses the correspondence of this painting with the one opposite, thus leading the PAGE 34 spectator to a parallel reading of the scenes, which is then extended to all the frescoes on the walls. In the right background is a sermon of Christ, and on the left a sermon of John the Baptist.

The second fresco, the work of Botticelli, is devoted to the *Temptations of* PAGE 41 *Christ*, which strangely, although they are the main subject of the picture – the title *Temptatio Ieso Christi latoris evangelicae legis* seems to refer to them – are represented in three successive episodes in the background. In the foreground is depicted a sacrificial rite which some have interpreted as the Purification of the Leper, while others see in it a symbolic content which transcends the " historical " significance of the scene – the priest is supposed to be Moses, representative of the old law by which the offering of blood is made, and the young acolyte is supposed to be Christ, the bearer of evangelic law, destined to redeem humanity by the sacrifice of his own blood.

The following painting, the only one remaining by Ghirlandaio, represents the PAGE 42 *Calling of the First Apostles*, and is divided inno a series of three scenes, of which the two in the background depict respectively the Calling of Peter and Andrew and the Calling of James and John. In the foreground are Christ and the kneeling figures of Andrew and Peter; the latter is made to stand out, as also in the *Handing over of the Keys*, as if to emphasize his role as Christ's successor. The Redeemer, who is obviously represented as the leader of the people "congregated" under the new law, dominates the center of the picture, as PAGE 36 Moses in the fresco opposite. The correspondence of meanings uniting the two paintings is stressed by the title, *Congregatio popoli legem evangelicam accepturi.*

PAGE 7 There follows the *Sermon on the Mount*, in which Christ takes on the character of legislator, as is stressed by the title *Promulgatio evangelicae legis per Christum.* The old law, delivered by Jahweh to Moses on Mt. Sinai, is thus contrasted with the law of the Beatitudes given by the Redeemer in his sermon. To the side is depicted the miracle of the Healing of the Leper. The fresco is swarming with figures, the work of Cosimo Rosselli, but the splendid landscape, cut across by a duck in flight, was painted, as Vasari records, by Piero di Cosimo.

The fifth panel, the most important of the series for its symbolic content, repre- PAGE 42 sents the *Handing over of the Keys* and is considered the masterpiece of Perugino, although some see the hand of Signorelli in some of the figures of Apostles. The scene, like the one opposite of the *Punishment of Corah*, is set in a city landscape – a great square, dominated by a domed building to the sides of which are symmetrically placed two triumphal arches, faithful copies of the Arch of PAGE 43 Constantine. In the background we note the Payment of the Tribute Money and the attempted Stoning of Christ, referred to in the title *Conturbatio Iesu Christi legislatoris*, which once again stresses the Redeemer's role as law-giver. The two figures to the right in the foreground, one with a set-square and the other with a sextant, are Giovannino de' Dolci and Baccio Pontelli; facing them is a figure with a thick mane of dark hair around his face, Perugino's self-portrait.

PAGE 44 The last fresco on this wall, the *Last Supper*, was again painted by Cosimo Rosselli with the help of Piero di Cosimo. The composition is quite traditional, with the exception of the addition of the still life and the two cats in the foreground. In the background are the Agony in the Garden, the Capture of Christ and the Crucifixion. The title *Replicatio legis evangelicae a Christo* refers to the main episode in which Christ, as in the corresponding scene of the Stories of Moses, assumes the role of priest as well as that of legislator, concluding the sequence of meanings that unifies the two cycles of frescoes.

Lost, as we have already said, is the masterpiece by Ghirlandaio depicting the *Resurrection of Christ*, repainted at the end of the sixteenth century by the Dutch painter Arrigo Paludano (Van der Broeck). There remains today only the title, although faded and incomplete, *Resurrectio et ascensio Christi evangelicae legis latoris.*

An iconographic program like that of the Sistine Chapel could certainly not have been left to the free will of the painters called to carry it out. It presents, in fact, many layers of meanings, which go from the traditional illustration of events from the Old and New Testament, to the pairing of episodes from each cycle on the basis of their typological similarity. Moses is in fact the best known precursor of Christ, and the necessity for exemplifying this theme, also in the titles, conditions the choice of episodes for both cycles. But alongside these meanings, which must have been obvious to the contemporaries of Sixtus IV, there is an evident intention to communicate another message, which becomes clear only on a careful reading of the two sets of stories. Moses is presented successively as leader, legislator and priest, and the same qualities are illustrated in the figure of Christ; of these aspects the titles stress especially the power to establish laws. Now, these qualities were handed down to Peter as the founder of the papacy in the fresco of the *Handing over of the Keys*, which is itself the PAGE 42 key to the interpretation of the whole wall decoration. It is no chance that in the background is shown the Payment of the Tribute Money, which alludes to the superiority of spiritual power over temporal, and the Arch of Constantine recurs twice – Constantine was the emperor who according to tradition officially sanctioned this power by his donation. To this we must add that the fresco opposite, the *Punishment of Corah*, contains a severe warning to all those who, PAGE 37 even from within the church, try to throw doubt on the authority of the papacy – a warning which becomes even more evident if we take into account the inscription painted on the triumphal arch, which once more reproduces that of Constantine.

Similar concepts to those expressed in the Stories in the Sistine Chapel – often, like the text of the inscription, drawn from the letter of St. Paul to the Hebrews – recur often in the writings of Sixtus IV, who at that time was fighting the threat of the Council of Basle which, manoeuvered by kings and bishops, aimed at weakening the powers of the papacy. This background explains also the presence of the gallery of " portraits " of the first thirty popes, which originally began with the images of Christ and Peter; it has the function, like the Stories below, of documenting the historical origins of papal power.

This programme is also the basis for the choice of a structural (in the sense of organization of interior space) and decorative pattern for the chapel based on the ancient proto-Christian basilicas, such as St. Paul's and St. Peter's, which had witnessed the foundation of the Church's power. Significantly, however, the Pope did not confine himself to a mere return to ancient times, but called some of the most " modern " artists of his own day to give his message a contemporary form. The content of this message was not altered by his successors; with the tapestries of Raphael (now in the Vatican Pinacoteca) and the frescoes of the ceiling and altar wall by Michelangelo it only became richer and more far-reaching.

Study for the ceiling of the Sistine Chapel London, British Museum

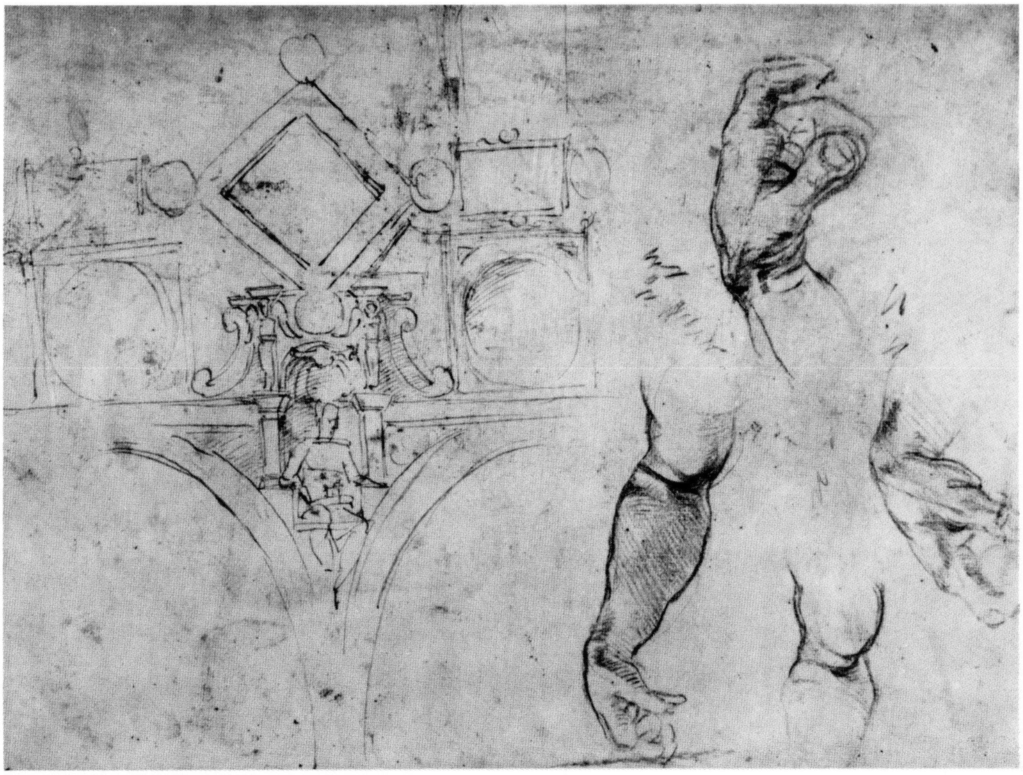

Study for the ceiling of the Sistine Chapel Courtesy of the Detroit Institute of Arts

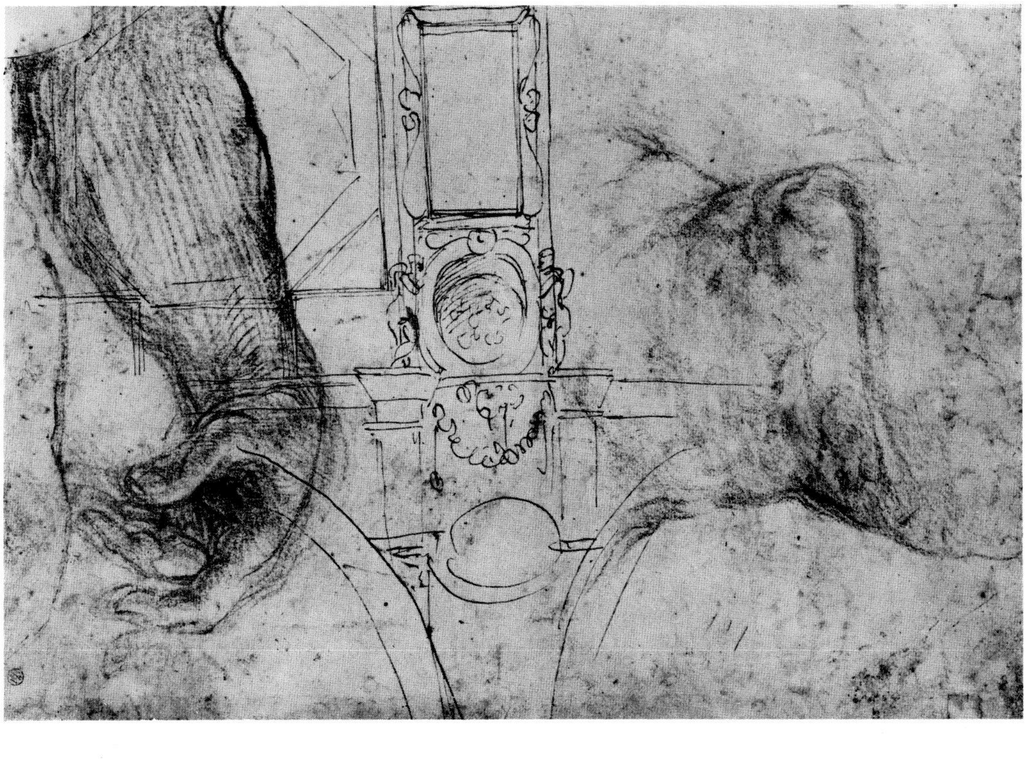

Lutz Heusinger

III. The Ceiling

The immediate successors to Sixtus IV (who died in 1484) left the Chapel as they found it. Pope Julius, of the same della Rovere family as Sixtus, ascended to the papacy in 1503. He soon decided to undertake an extensive addition to the decoration of the building with the painting of the vault. In 1506 he was already considering the plan, but not till 1508 did he commission Michelangelo to execute it. As we know from a letter of the artist, an ornamental decoration was intended, with pictures only of the twelve apostles. How the final, extremely detailed design, including more than 300 figures, came to be realized, we do not know but can only surmise.

In 1505 the Pope together with Michelangelo had planned a huge tomb for himself. It was to be surrounded by forty life-size statues and represent an allegory of the state of the world at the time. Perhaps excited by his search for a suitable setting for this monument, the Pope conceived the even more ambitious plan of finally building anew the First Church of the Christian world. The laying of the first stone of St. Peter's in April 1506 meant, however, for Michelangelo the end for the present of his work on the tomb, as all forces had then to be concentrated on the building of the church. Completely against his will, the Pope for the next two years kept him busy in Bologna on a bronze portrait statue. The creative energy dammed up in the artist during these years, and stirred by the work already begun on the powerful figures for the tomb, must have made the original design for the painting of the Sistine vault seem very disappointing to him. It is therefore not improbable that the initiative for the extension of the plan came from Michelangelo himself, as he asserts in a letter. The row of ancestors of Christ in the lunettes and spandrels creates a natural PAGE 85 link between the fifteenth century wall paintings and the vault. We cannot exclude the possibility that these ancestor paintings were in fact planned before 1483. Neither can the idea of covering the central fields of the vault with the images of Christian cosmology and the stories of the first men surprise us within the framework of the popes' chapel. It is harder to answer the question of the reason for the scenes from the Old Testament in the four corner spandrels, the meaning of the prophets and sibyls, and the effect intended in the various decorative figures.

Michelangelo insisted all his life that he was a sculptor, not a painter. After the commission for the Sistine ceiling had replaced that for the tomb, if his letters of the years 1508-12 can be relied on, he was reserved, bitter, and subject to outbursts of violence. Right at the beginning of the work, in 1508, he discharged

Study for the ceiling of the Sistine Chapel
London, British Museum

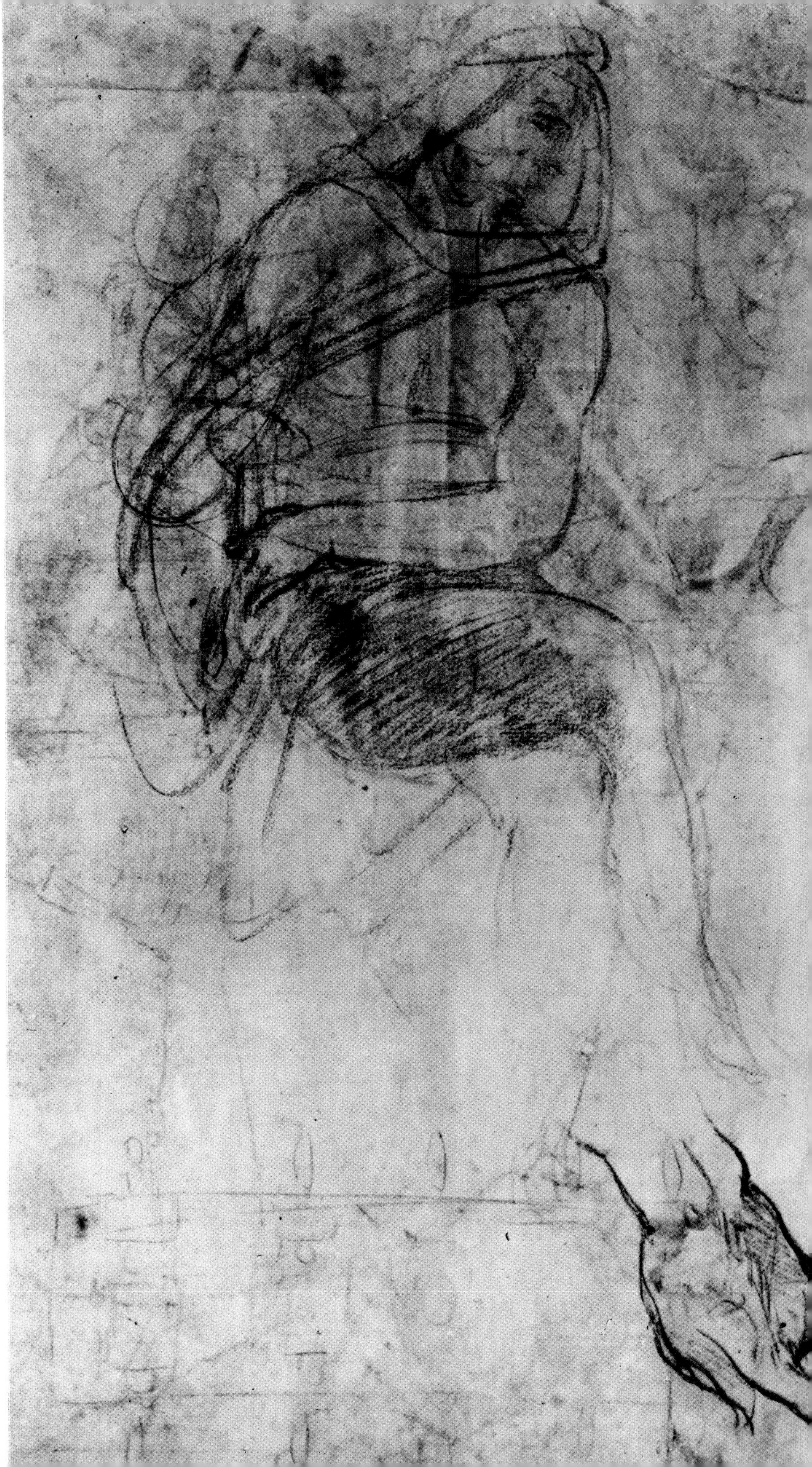

a group of assistants whom he had brought from Florence because he did not trust the Romans. Then by the 31st of October 1512, in four periods of several months each, he carried out the whole work. Exactly how much of it was done by assistants is not known. By Autumn 1509 the first three big frescos with all adjoining decorative parts were done, and by August 1510 the next two. Then followed several months during which the Pope, who stayed on in Bologna, kept him waiting for money. The last four big frescos were painted between January and August 1511, and finally in 1512 the row of lunettes. We are struck by the fact that the artist began his work, counter to historical or chronological order, not with the *Creation of Light* above the altar but with the *Deluge* and the two Noah frescos at the east end above the entrance. These paintings, whose composition is denser and whose subject cosmologically later, probably seemed to him easier exercises, less trying to his inexperience. And that he was lacking at the outset in the necessary experience for the execution of monumental frescos, he himself recognized and several times stressed.

We still have two sketches by Michelangelo of the plan in its early stages, with PAGE 11
the twelve apostles. The earlier one, now in London, shows a quite traditional fifteenth centrury design, in which circular and square fields alternate and the apostles are placed in conch-shaped niches. The later sketch, preserved in Detroit, already shows some essential elements of the ceiling as it was executed. The thrones of the apostles have become the starting points for bridge-like bands across the vault, dividing it into octagonal fields. The decorative effect has clearly become subordinate here to the effect of the pictorial area, though in this sketch the artist is also studying the possibilities of the ornamental framework. When he came to carry it out, Michelangelo decided, with the use of a yellowish colour, to give it the characteristics of massive stone. So today over and between the spandrels of the vault rises a compact and uninterrupted stone wall, which is joined to the surface of the vault above by a powerfully molded cornice. From the projections rise massive stone bands, dividing the ceiling rhythmically into large and small fields, the settings for the great scenes. The relationship between painted and materially constructed architecture is left intentionally ill-defined. Next to the *Drunkenness of Noah* and the *Creation of Light* appear small strips of blue sky, creating the illusion that the vault is open. The scenes themselves, however, are not meant to give the illusion of occurring in a distant sky. Correspondingly, there is no common, overall focal point, as the architecture, the single scenes, and the decorative figures are all presented with separate and independent perspective structures.

There can be no doubt that, as with the wall frescos, the plan of the ceiling had also been considered and approved by the Pope, and that also in the early sixteenth century the artist, even if personally highly respected, was very strongly bound by the dictates of his patrons. But all the same Michelangelo's paintings show considerably more of the artist's personality than Perugino's *Baptism of Christ*, for example, shows of his. It is therefore necessary to ascertain as much as possible about Michelangelo's character and the circumstances of his life at the time when he was painting the ceiling. Undoubtedly the most important source are the letters which he wrote during these years, and especially those to his family. They continually revert to the question of how the money earned by him can be invested most usefully and most favourably for his father and brothers. If he hears of ill-considered spending he loses his temper and writes threateningly to Florence. On the other hand, a mistaken estimate of a political danger leads him to the precipitate advice to his family to abandon everything and go into exile in Siena. These impulsive reactions become understandable if one hears what Michelangelo says about his personal life in Rome. Since he mistrusts the Romans, his human contacts are restricted almost completely to the Florentine man-servant who looks after his household. He has no helpful or relaxing encounters with equals, and he has not the habit, so common at that time, of losing himself in the writings of the past. In contrast to Bramante, who next door to him was directing the building of the new St. Peter's and gathered impressions from every possible direction, to the point where he could hardly work them all out satisfactorily, Michelangelo seems to have concentrated completely on the realization of the established plan for the vault. His work can therefore hardly be explained—as has often been tried—as based on a rich knowledge of Christian theological or Neo-Platonic sources; it has rather to be looked at and interpreted with the greatest immediacy.

IV. The Old Testament Scenes

Taken in chronological order, the first five scenes of the vault show events from Genesis, the sixth the *Fall*, the last three the *Sacrifice of Noah*, the *Deluge*, and *Noah's Drunkenness*. The four corner spandrels also show incidents from the Old P.P. 62 - 65 Testament—the *Brazen Serpent*, *The Punishment of Haman*, the *Death of Holofernes* and the *Death of Goliath*. These four scenes, therefore, show God's condemnation of his slanderers or aggressors. In the Middle Ages these incidents represented at the same time symbolic victories of particular virtues over vices—David as strength and bravery over Goliath as greed, Judith as moderation over Holophernes as presumption and excess, Haman and the Jewish people of the Brazen Serpent examples again of presumption. As well as these immediate meanings the frescos in the corner spandrels, in accordance with their position, make the connection between the wall frescos and the vault paintings; Moses is the hero in the incident of the Brazen Serpent, and David stands as precursor and ancestor of Christ in the Goliath scene. The relationship between Moses and Christ on the one hand and the popes on the other hand, is also the underlying theme of the fifteenth century frescos on the lower walls.

PAGE 47

If we follow Michelangelo's order of working, the fresco of the *Deluge* is the first one to consider. The top, right-hand corner of this painting was damaged in 1797 by an explosion of gun-powder in the Castel Sant'Angelo, so that a strong and leafy tree which counter-balanced the group of people on the mountain on the left of the small island is missing. Michelangelo has depicted the moment of the biblical incident when only a few landmarks are still showing above the livid grey water of the flood. It is not these landmarks, however, but the people, who give definition to the scene. And they are not represented as lost sinners but are seen in gestures of care for each other, helping and protecting. Only in the background, around the boat and especially on Noah's Ark, are brutal scenes being played out among the threatened. This strikes us as all the more strange as the Ark, with the dove and Noah on the watch, is obviously the place of survival. Right at this point, in the figures of fighting people, Michelangelo describes the despair of the flood and the struggles of the sinful, making clear to us his terrible conception of the survival of sin and conflict with the survival of even one single person.

PAGE 46

In the biblical story the drunken Noah, fallen asleep after hard work on the land, was discovered naked by his son Ham. Ham's two brothers, whom he tells of this, cover their father's nakedness while Ham mocks him. That " nakedness " here is not to be confused with nudity has been clearly shown by the artist in the fact that the sons are not clothed either. The lesson of this incident is in fact stated in their very nudity, for the body of Ham with its stooping shoulders and feminine, rounded belly appears weak and useless.

PAGE 54

Whether the scene of sacrifice shows the thank offering of Noah after leaving the Ark or some other sacrifice from the Old Testament is still being disputed. Unclear points like the entrails in the hand of the standing youth, which cannot have been taken from the slaughtered animal, or the " prompting " attitude of the old woman behind the altar, justify the uncertainty with regard to this painting. Apparently Michelangelo did not succeed here in representing more than the genre-like external characteristics of the incident.

P.P. 55 - 57

The *Fall* and the *Expulsion from Paradise* are painted as only a sculptor could paint them. All scenery is excluded; only the figures of the first human couple, in two statuesque groups, illustrate and interpret the incidents. On the left the two figures, contrary to biblical ideas of the temptation of Adam by Eve, are fused into one group, within which however their gestures are differentiated; Adam is aggressively grasping, Eve quietly, almost lazily accepting. About the face and body of the latter figure absolutely everything has been said by art historians that can be said about a woman—incarnation of female beauty, symbol of female lust, yearning and sensitive, gigantic and demanding. The group on the right-hand side, which is strongly related to Masaccio's *Expulsion* in the Church of the Carmine in Florence, shows, in accordance with the paternalistic notions of Christianity, Adam in a gesture of defence and Eve huddling under his protection.

P.P. 48, 49

In the *Creation of Eve* the tree trunk, Adam's uncomfortable position, and the

Study for the ceiling of the Sistine Chapel London, British Museum

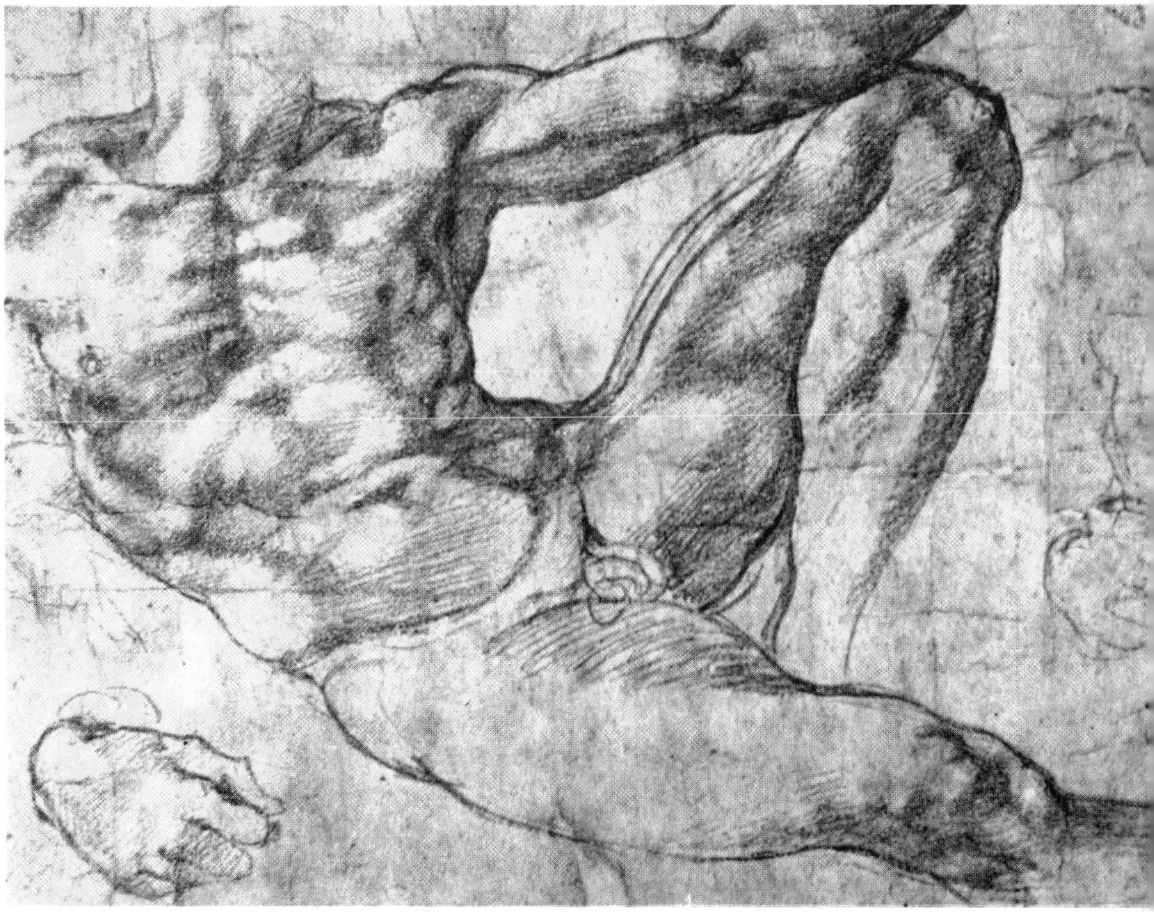

unsteady stance of the mighty God figure, have all yet to be rightly understood and explained. However, we will hesitate to be content with ascribing these only to the inability of the artist if we observe how the act of creation itself is represented, with the greatest artistic power and intensity. The glances and the gestures of the hands are all that reveal how Michelangelo conceived this cosmological act. God compels the woman to rise, and she turns to him with a prayer-like gesture and slightly parted lips, without however at all understanding what is happening.

P.P. 50 - 53 According to the Old Testament account, the *Creation of Adam* consists of two acts; his body is formed of dust, and the breath of God gives him a soul. Michelangelo has represented only the second, and this in a thoroughly a-christian way. Adam lies, already a complete and individual being, in a leisurely position inclining only his head in an attitude of yearning towards God, who hovers surrounded by angels before the grey void of the sky. The desire of mankind for the touch of God thus appears as independent and willed; the creation of Adam becomes a fulfilment of this longing, not a creation of something out of nothing. The truly marvellous woman with wide and almost fearful eyes below the arm of the creator can best be understood as an image of Eve, naturally less as a Platonic " idea " of the as yet uncreated woman, than as a goal of man's desire.

The motif of the hovering God was used by Michelangelo in the last three central frescos in increasing measure for the representation of creative power. In the *Separation of Land and Water*, the outstretched hands and the strongly foreshor- PAGE 58 tened body created an immediate impression of the act as described in the Bible. The fresco of the *Creation of the Stars*, with the creation of plant life on the left- P.P. 59, 60 hand side, is related to the first episode in being based on a rotatory movement in which the power of the act of creation as such, rather than what is created, is significant and evident. The combining of different themes in a single composition, as in the *Creation of the Stars* makes quite clear that what was above all important for Michelangelo at this late stage of his work on the ceiling was neither the ornamental framework nor any of the decorative elements, but only the "human" figure, whether as creating god or as naked youth. Only the figure defines place; there is never a predomination of space or of composition. This becomes even clearer in the arrangement of the fresco of the *Creation of Light*, chronologically first, but last to be painted. Cosmological ideas of the PAGE 61 ancients, according to which God as pure form unites in a mighty whirlwind movement with primordial matter, thus immediately giving it reality, seem undoubtedly to be illustrated here; and this although Michelangelo cannot have been very familiar with the Aristotelian and Neo-Platonic thought of the classical Renaissance generation. We can deduce that this philosophy did not remain the property of a few highly cultured people, but must have corresponded to an attitude to life wide-spread at the time. This spirit of the times, as Michelangelo's Last Judgment shows, was to be. change profoundly within a few years.

The first story of the tomb of Pope Julius was supposed according to the original plan to be surrounded by representations of the virtues and the arts. The virtues were to be depicted here not as ideal female figures as was the custon at the times but as groups fighting with the vices. The same tendency not to represent virtue as free and idealized is shown in the scenes in the corner spandrels. David, PAGE 62 against all custom and tradition, is shown not as triumphant victor, but still in battle. Judith and her maid appear not safe on their way back to their city, PAGE 63 as for example in Botticelli, but on the threshold of Holofernes' room, while they still have before them the dangerous journey through the enemy camp. In the Haman spandrel the whole episode is presented in three single scenes, PAGE 64 in which Michelangelo's special interest is obviously in the moment when Haman's infamous intentions are discovered (the left-hand corner of the painting). The artist hardly ever again achieved the height of excitement expressed in the figures of Esther, Ahasuerus and Haman.

How far away Michelangelo was from the spirit of the Pope's plans for the ceiling, we can see in the *Brazen Serpent*. Here, where through Moses the connection PAGE 65 to the earlier wall frescoes and thus to the papacy should have been brought out, the figure of the Jewish leader, if it is shown at all, is completely lost in the terrifying depiction of the event.

The maturity of these four spandrel frescos, for example the composition of the

Judith scene, suggests that they were realized during the last period of the work, at the same time as the lunettes.

V. The Decorative Figures

The various interpretations which up to the present day have been given to the Sistine vault are particularly contradictory when it comes to the explanation of the decorative figures. Two contemporaries and biographers of Michelangelo, P.P. 66 - 69 Vasari and Condivi, saw them as " Ignudi ", nude youths, symbolizing the golden age which had dawned with the reign of Julius II. Somewhat similarly they are also interpreted as representing the fine arts, their " Grecian " character symbolizing the return of ancient art. Lastly and most complicated there is the explanation given by recent researchers into the work of Michelangelo. According to these, the planner and Michelangelo himself were thinking here of the various spheres of being, as they are distinguished for example in Platonic philosophy. The human microcosm is supposed to consist of three degrees, " natura corporale " (body), " anima razionale " (soul) and " natura intellettiva " (intellect), each of which has its own life-principle. Carrying over this scheme to the paintings of the vault, all the decorative figures are seen in relation to the prophets and sibyls; the putti with the name tablets as " natura corporale ", the figures beside the seers as " anima razionale ", and the Ignudi as " natura intellettiva ". It apparently fits in with this explanation that the putti with the tablets match in colour the darker area with the ancestors of Christ in the lunettes and spandrels, while the rest belong to the lighter zone of the seers and Old Testament scenes. Not explained in this design, however, are the " marble " putti-caryatids which flank the thrones of the seers, and the " bronze " youths above the spandrels. But in just this fact we may find a further explanation for the decorative figures, according to which they embody the forces at work in the real and painted architecture. The consideration of the decorative figures is most fruitful if we ask first what their practical function is. In the case of the putti with the name tablets of the seers it is quite clear, as also with the putti-caryatids. The function of the Ignudi is more difficult to comprehend. They sit on stone blocks above the projections of the cornice, fixed in their place by the heavy garlands and " bronze " shields in painted relief which they are holding. Little putti were used in the same way for example by Donatello or Michelangelo's teacher Ghirlandaio, and it is certainly correct to see the nude youths, like their putti predecessors, as above all decorative, secondary figures, meant to celebrate the particular quality of the events to which they are related, triumph or sorrow as it may be. If then the garlands of oakleaves are an allusion to the oak in the coat of arms of the della Rovere family, to which both Sixtus and Julius belonged—the popes who did most for the Sistine Chapel—the Ignudi are fully explained; they can be compared also to the many boys and girls who inevitably accompanied festival and triumphal processions at the time.

If however we stop to study the single Ignudi, they seem almost to be a catalogue of the variety of human physical and psychological possibilities. We find the mournfully sensitive and the choleric, the lucid Apollonian and the sensuous Dionysian. There are also great differences in the quality of their activity. While many of the youths seem to us to be dedicating a natural amount of effort to their work, others are almost fighting with the garlands. If we are looking for the style called Mannerism somewhere in the years following 1500, we can find it being prepared here; the discrepancy between bodily activity, physical being and spiritual expression is already present, the one exaggerated to make the other possible. We perceive that for the followers of Michelangelo only one more step was needed to bring this discrepancy to the fore, and so to break with the Renaissance ideal of classical balance and unity. P.P. 66 - 69

As the significance of the Ignudi goes far beyond that of their immediate function, so also the putti-caryatids express more than their practical reason for being. In most cases there are a boy and a girl together, playing, teasing each other or fighting over a piece of garment. Michelangelo thus clearly shows, even in these little figures, that the structure of the painted architecture is never important to him in itself, but only for the hardness and solidity of its stone-work as a background for the existence of the independent beings he creates. PAGE 78

The bronze-coloured youths in the triangles above the spandrels form a special world to themselves. The fiery tone of their skin in itself gives them an inhuman quality. The ram skulls, often used for decoration on altars of sacrifice, and the violet curtains over pale golden frames, surround them with an underworldly atmosphere. But they should probably be interpreted not as genii of death but, taken as a whole, as incarnations of unconscious human life, the life of the instincts. Only in this way can we explain why many of them are raving in fury, others lie completely relaxed (in single cases similar to the later figures on the Medici tombs in Florence), and others seem to be fettered, with painful contortions of their bodies. What these figures, above the ancestors of Christ and next to the Seers, mean in relationship to the whole ceiling has not yet been convincingly explained. PAGE 85

The reliefs on the " bronze shields " which the Ignudi are holding refer to accounts from the Second Book of Kings and the Second Book of Samuel. Four of them illustrate the story of David, three the ruin of the godless tribe of Ahab, one the destruction of the heathen cult of Baal, and the last the sacrifice of Isaac. The reliefs are painted " al fresco " with a brown colour, and touched up when dry with gold. Why one of the medallions was left plain is not known. The two medallions illustrated here show the *Death of Absalom* and the *Destruction of the Tribe of Ahab*. Where Michelangelo got the idea of adding " bronze shields " to his design, how the single medallions fit into the general plan of the ceiling, and to what extent assistants may have worked here, remain, like many other questions, yet to be clarified. P.P. 69, 70

VI. The Prophets and Sibyls - The Ancestors of Christ

Since the late Middle Ages it had been traditional to bring together in one cycle Christian prophets and heathen sibyls; and often to unite this to representations of the ancestors of Christ. The most famous example in Italy of a cycle uniting prophets and sibyls must at Michelangelo's time have been the one by Giovanni Pisano, from before 1300, on the facade of the Cathedral in Siena. The reasons for the choice of the seers represented in the Sistine vault can only be surmised. The presence of the four great prophets, Isaiah, Jeremiah, Ezekiel and Daniel, can be taken for granted. Zechariah is supposed to have been depicted over the entrance to the Chapel as the prophet of Palm Sunday, as it was the Pope's custom to make a festive entry there on Palm Sunday after distributing palm branches. Jonah and the whale, as symbol of the Resurrection, seem to be in their rightful place above the altar. The presence of Joel, the prophet of Whitsuntide, can be explained by the fact that the Whitsun vigil was held in the chapel, and during Conclave the mass of the Holy Ghost was sung there. Why precisely the Roman sibyl, Tiburtina, should be missing from among her companions in art, is just as hard to understand as why the Delphian, Erythrean, Cumaean, Persian and Libyan sibyls should have been chosen to be represented.

Like the bronze-coloured youths and the ancestors of Christ, the figures of the seers can be fully understood only if we consider them as a group. Only then the differences between them stand out clearly, and each figure reveals its individuality. As each figure is depicted from a different point of vision, so also
PAGE 71 there is no logical progression from one to the other. *Zechariah* is portrayed turning over the leaves of his folio volume, searching or lost in thought. The power of the figure lies not in the action or in any inner agitation, but only in its outward appearance, especially in the full and tranquil drapery of the robes. A different type
PAGE 72 of experience is depicted in the *Delphian Sibyl.* Her torso is raised in an abrupt movement and her head turns forwards. The eyes are wide open and turned even further, as if a voice has reached her from the right while she was reading in the open scroll. The powerful swing of her movements is almost too strongly emphasized by the curves of the scroll and the robe. Her lips are slightly parted for the prophetic words to come. Michelangelo has caught in this figure the ecstatic moment at which the unhearable is about to be heard and revealed.

PAGE 73 What is most impressive about *Joel* is his noble face. The first and powerful excitement which has seized him while he reads shows in the contrasting position of the legs, suggesting equally stillness and tension.

PAGE 74 The figure of *Isaiah* has classical manly beauty, intensity and energy. There is a clear unfolding of action in this painting. The prophet has been reading, has put the book on one side to lean on it, holding it open with his little finger, and has immediately heard the voice of the boy behind him. He has lifted his head from his hand and turned to the right. In a moment his eyes will have to follow where the child is pointing. Leaving aside the action, this fresco is a composition developed out of contrasts—the heads of man and boy, the strong swing of the robes on the left and the relaxed attitude of the body on the right. This contrast is interpreted as representing the resistance of the prophet to the compelling voice of God.

An explanation for the small companions of the Seers can best be given by taking the examples of *Isaiah* and the *Erythrean Sibyl*. In both cases the directly or symbolically represented inspiration is personified in these companion figures. P.P. 74, 75

With the muscular fullness of her body and her great age, the *Cumaean Sibyl* is at the same time witch-like and gigantic. Ovid recounts that Apollo in scorn condemned her to a life of a thousand years; but the power of this woman seems completely unbroken. PAGE 76

Among all the seer figures, *Ezekiel* is the one who seems most overwhelmed by his vision. The scroll and garment swing wildly, and the the body is in violent movement. The right hand is open in a gesture of refusal, though the eyes are turned in the same direction, where the angelic, Leonardo-like boy is pointing. The contrast between the young and innocent face of the boy and the wild features and hair of the prophet adds to the impression of his greatness and power. PAGE 77

Daniel, the *Libyan* and the *Persian Sibyls* are all occupied in various ways with writing; the Libyca gives the effect of a Manneristic genre study. Perhaps the most fascinating, certainly the gayest, of the putti-caryatids are those beside Daniel. It becomes quite clear here that they should be seen as independent beings, without reference to the seer figures, providing a festive, life-affirming accompaniment to the lofty gallery of superhuman personages. P.P. 78, 84, 79 PAGE 84 PAGE 78

The most tragic figure of the group is certainly the prophet *Jeremiah*. The uncouthness of this man, whose existence appears to be almost entirely physical, makes a very strong impression, heightened by the attitude of the accompanying figure, apparently a woman, with its sadly sunk head. The thoughtful pose, which Rodin repeated centuries later in his figure of the " Thinker ", intensifies further the impression of isolated and fettered bodily being in this man, in whose image, more than any other from the ceiling, Michelangelo reveals his vision of himself. P.P. 80, 81

The form of *Jonah*, half-reclining, seems almost to burst out of its place in the architectural structure. Michelangelo is certainly referring to the moment in which the prophet has just escaped from the sea and the jaw of the whale, which is typologically the moment of resurrection. Every detail is in violent movement; the face is still turned upwards, questioning and pointing at the same time. The artist could hardly have created a more extreme contrast to the figure of Zechariah on the opposite wall over the entrance. P.P. 82, 83

Going right along the spandrels and lunettes and alternating from one side of

Study for the ceiling of the Sistine Chapel
London, British Museum

the chapel to the other are the ancestors of Christ, in the order given by St. Matthew. Since on the name tablets in the lunettes appear from one to three names, independently of whether or not there is a spandrel, the certain identification of the single figures is almost impossible; and the more so because Michelangelo has not based these paintings on stories from the Bible. It hardly fits in with the biblical account that in the spandrels families are represented, with the woman in the foreground. We have to conclude that Michelangelo wanted to give here the most comprehensive picture possible of human life, without reference to historical sources; in the spandrels "Woman" and in the lunettes "Man" are portrayed at various moments of their lives, as various types, involved in various experiences. The parents of the sleeping future king *Josias*, for example, are shown asleep, but while the man with his coarse face is PAGE 86 quite isolated, the mother still embraces her child as she sleeps. The family of the little *Uzziah* seem to have collapsed exhausted. Only with a great effort the PAGE 87 small, pale woman supports the pressure of the child at her breast, without the father in the background being able to help her in any way; the scene has the effect of a representation of the eternal renewal of suffering through birth. A different impression is given by the picture of the families of *Eleazar and Mathan*, PAGE 88 in which the fathers appear to be disturbed by their children. The figures of *Jacob*, *Jechonias* and *Joshaphat* are depicted with biting immediacy. *David* appears P.P. 88, 89 more manly, a more impressive leader; in the painting a maid approaches timidly to bring him a meal. The last two lunettes before the altar wall—where before it was painted over for the *Last Judgment* the ancestor cycle began—show a young king in the company of a woman; in both cases the theme of two young PAGE 89 people approaching each other is treated with humourous directness. But the heights of seriousness and tragic piquancy reached by Michelangelo in this series of figures can best be seen in *Boaz*; clutching the handle of his stick on which PAGE 90 his wan image is sculpted, with futile energy and rage he symbolizes the hopelessness of human efforts.

VII. The Last Judgment

Soon after the completion of the painting of the ceiling Pope Julius II died. His successor Leo X, the first Medici pope, ordered in 1516 from Raphael ten designs for tapestries with the stories of the apostles, which were carried out by Pieter van Aelst of Brussels. At Christmas 1519 they were hung up for the first time before the painted curtains in the lowest zone of the chapel. Today they are in the seventh room of the Vatican gallery. For Michelangelo the rule of Leo X brought great misfortune. In 1513, shortly after the death of Julius II,

Study for the ceiling of the Sistine Chapel
London, British Museum

he had concluded a new contract with his heirs for the tomb already planned in 1505. But Leo very soon wanted to make use of Michelangelo's artistic talents for himself, and commissioned him with the building of the facade of the Medici church in Florence, San Lorenzo. Just when, after hard work in the quarries of Carrara, this project was entering the decisive phase, the Pope changed his mind. It must have been in 1521, shortly before his death, that he made Michelangelo break off the work on San Lorenzo and commissioned him with the building of the Medici Chapel.

A decisive part in this new project was taken by Giulio dei Medici, who in 1523 was to become, with the name of Clement VII, the second Medici pope. The reign of Clement VII brought with it political events which had a profound effect on Michelangelo's life. In spite of support from the papacy, in 1527 the Medicis were driven out of Florence, so that the artist had to cease his work on the Medici tombs. In the same year with the Sack of Rome the most terrible plundering of modern times occurred in that city. In 1529 Spanish troops moved

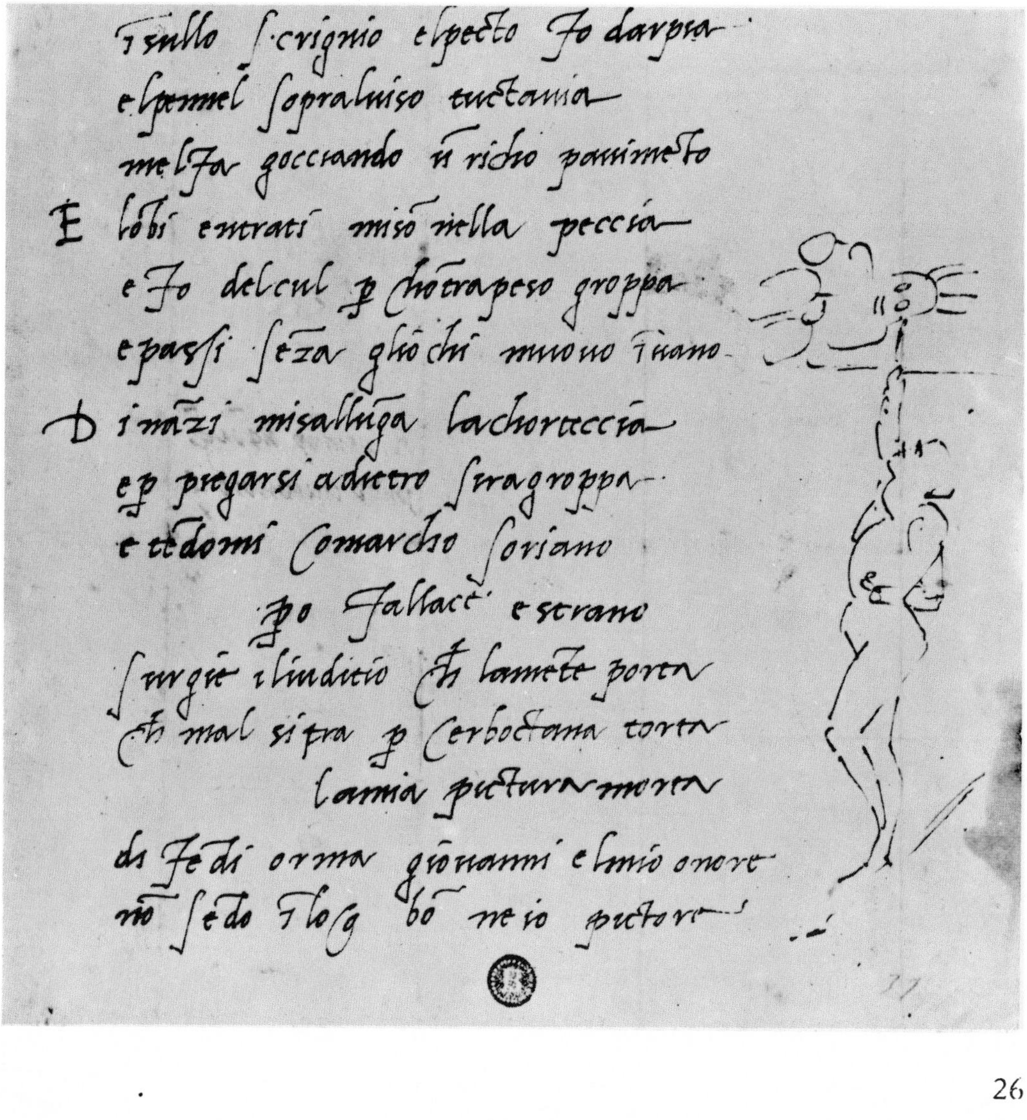
i sullo scrignio elpecto fo darpia
elpennel sopraluiso tuctavia
melfa gocciando u richo pavimẽto
E lobi entrati miso nella peccia
e fo delcul p chõtrapeso groppa
epassi sẽza gliochi muovo i vano
D inazi misallunga lachorteccia
ep piegarsi adietro siragroppa
e tedomi comarcho soriano
po fallace e strano
surgie iliuditio che lamete porta
chi mal si tra p cerbottana torta
lamia pictura morta
di fedi orma giovanni elmio onore
no sedo ilocho bo ne io pictore

Sonnet in Michelangelo's handwriting with sketch of a figure painting a ceiling, detail Florence, Buonarroti Archive

against the Republic of Florence to restore the Medicis to their hereditary rights, and Michelangelo fought against them as brilliant builder and director of city fortifications. The city was nevertheless taken, and the artist had once more to return to the service of his enemies the Medicis, and work on their Chapel. In 1553, when the preparations of the Council of Trent for defeating the Protestants were well under way, Clement VII decided to call Michelangelo to Rome for a new project in the Sistine Chapel, although his work in Florence was far from completed. The developments of the historical situation had matured in the Pope the decision to decorate the altar wall of the papal chapel with a huge *Last Judgment*, and a fresco of the *Resurrection* corresponding to it on the entrance wall. But the Pope died in 1534, before the work could be begun. However, his successor Paul III Farnese immediately renewed Michelangelo's commission; and in April 1535 the scaffolding was put up in front of the altar wall. More than six years later, on the 31st of October, 1541, the new work was unveiled. Why the Resurrection fresco was not carried out we can only surmise. Other projects, especially the two frescos in the Pauline Chapel of the Vatican, completed in 1540, and the tomb of Pope Julius, for which the heirs would wait no longer, must have appeared more urgent; but in any case, in the particular historical situation of the time, a representation of the Resurrection probably seemed less necessary than the Last Judgment.

Michelangelo from 1515 on was too closely bound to the papacy not to have been deeply and personally affected by these crises, and not only the Reformation and the Sack of Rome, but also the progressive change in outlook from the time of the wall frescos up to that of the *Last Judgment*. The *Last Judgment*—almost unique on an altar wall—was in fact conceived to show the equality of all men before the last and most important event in the Christian epic of salvation.

Besides the direct influence which general developments had on Michelangelo, during the time he was working on the Last Judgment fresco he was strongly affected also by a personal experience which led him to interpret in an individual manner the most important problems of his time. In 1538 he came to know Vittoria Colonna, a highly cultured poetess who was one of the spiritual leaders of a circle urging reform from within the Catholic church. The basic conviction of this circle was that only God's mercy and not human achievement is definitive in the Christian life. The effect of this way of thinking on Michelangelo can be seen in the drawings which he did for Vittoria Colonna. In his youthful Roman *Pietà* (in St. Peter's) the expression of immortal beauty was still his chief aim; now a page with a drawing of the Pietà bears the line from Dante " Non vi si pensa quanto sangue costa " (One does not think of how much blood it costs.) This could also have been the motto of Michelangelo's life in the time between Sixtus IV and Clement VII.

Some of this personal and general development can be quite clearly seen in a
PAGE 91 comparision of the Sistine ceiling and the *Last Judgment*. Architectural arrangement, and with it all sense of predominant or underlying order, is lacking in the *Last Judgment*. The colour range has become even narrower in comparison

with the ceiling. Only once in the *Last Judgment* does Michelangelo put colour in first place—the sulphurous yellow behind Christ, hardly distinguishable as light, which marks the centre out of which the event, as a whole and in all its details, arises and evolves. The irregular blue of the background and the brown-green tones of the bodies hardly have the effect of colours. We see only human bodies, which are defined in place, form and gesture only by the power emanating from Christ. Christ is portrayed in an attitude which cannot be correctly described as either sitting or stepping forward. His right arm is raised, but points towards the left, where a frightful struggle is going on between the angels and the Damned who are striving to rise into Heaven, and sends the Damned swirling down into the depths. On the other side his almost unmoving left hand creates a suction which with equal force draws upwards the bodies of the Elect. The Last Judgment appears then not as the pronouncement of a sentence, as a mental act, but as the execution of it. Up to the time of Michelangelo, the idea of subjection to a sentence had been reserved to the Damned, while the saved were gently led along by friendly angels. But here Michelangelo has represented God's mercy as something just as terrible and just as inexorably powerful as his condemnation.

PAGE 92

Michelangelo's vision of himself during the years he was working on the *Last Judgment* is illustrated especially clearly in the two self portraits which he included in his fresco. The more important and more striking one is the face of the torn off skin which St. Bartholomew is holding in his left hand. The artist must have been referring directly to the many sorrows which he believed he owed to the wickedness of others, and indirectly to an idea which he later illustrated in the Pauline Chapel, between 1542 and 1550. Against all tradition he placed the fresco of the conversion of Paul opposite that of the crucifixion of Peter. We can only conclude that in his feeling conversion could be sealed only by martyrdom, and interpret in the same sense his portraying his own features on the symbol of the martyrdom of the apostles, the skin of Bartholomew. The second self portrait is the old man at the bottom left-hand edge of the fresco, who is helping the people to rise from the grave and encouraging them. The desire projected by the artist in this self portrait needs no explaining.

PAGE 96

Unusual, and probably again an idea of Michelangelo's rather than of the Pope his patron, is the monumental setting given to the symbols of the Passion. We understand from this that Michelangelo wished to depict in the highest place not the perfect harmony of Heaven awaiting the Elect, but something quite different—what the appearance of God as Man in the world brought to fulfilment, the conquering of human sin, and what this victory cost. And he conveys this with a directness which allows no further possible symbolic explanation. Conflict and suffering in full force are recalled again at the last moment. The meaning of the two lunettes can perhaps most easily be rightly understood by going back again to the Pietà and Crucifixion drawings which the artist did in these years for Vittoria Colonna.

Study for the Last Judgment, Florence, Uffizi - Gabinetto Disegni

In the bottom and last part of the *Last Judgment* Michelangelo worked on two images from literature. In the vision of Ezekiel it is written that on the last day skeletons shall come out of their graves and be clothed in new flesh, and in

PAGE 95

Dante we find the lines: "Charon, the spirit with eyes of fire, / has gathered them all together with a sign, / fells with his oar any who still hesitate." Accordingly we see on the left the skeletons rising up, and on the other side the terrible Charon with his oar. This was the end of the long process of decoration of the Sistine Chapel; nothing more has been added to this day.

Brief History of the Sistine Chapel

1277-1280	Reign of Pope Niccolò III (Giovanni Gaetano Orsini) who founded the « palatium novum » (the South and East wings of the existing Apostolic Palace) which included a « capella magna » that remained in use until 28-V-1473.
1475 (?)	The « capella magna » of Niccolò III destroyed to make way for the construction, on the same spot, of the Sistine Chapel during the pontificate of Sixtus IV (Francesco della Rovere).
1480 26-X-1481	Conclusion of the building of the Sistine Chapel Contract signed with Cosimo Rosselli, Domenico Ghirlandaio and Perugino for the decoration of the walls in the Sistine Chapel.
9-VIII-1483	First mass celebrated in the Chapel, for the anniversary of the election of Sixtus IV.
15-VIII-1483	On the Feast of the Assumption of the Virgin, Pope Sixtus IV solemnly dedicates the Chapel to the Madonna.
1484-1492	Pontificate of Innocent VIII (G. B. Cibo), during which the Sacristy along the West façade of the Chapel is built.
10-V-1508	Commissioned by Pope Julius II (Giuliano della Rovere), Michelangelo begins the preparatory drawings for the frescoes of the Sistine Ceiling.
January 1509	Michelangelo begins frescoing the Ceiling above the entrance.
September 1509	By this date the first three stories (Stories of Noah) at the top of the Ceiling are finished as are the figures in the adjacent area.
August 1510	By this month the Fall and the Creation of Eve and the surrounding figures are finished. (De Campos and De Tolnay give the month of September as the time of the completion of the Fall).
January-August 1511	The last four stories of Genesis on the Ceiling are finished together with the surrounding figures.
October 1511- October 1512	The Ancestors of Christ are painted in the lunettes along the walls.
1-XI-1512	All Saints' Day, Julius II consecrates the frescoes with a mass in the Chapel.
1515	Leo X (Giovanni dei Medici) orders from Pieter van Aelst in Brussels the weaving of tapestries to be used in the decoration of the Chapel. The cartoons for these tapestries (now to be found in the Victoria and Albert Museum in London) are by Raphael and the tapestries themselves now hang in the Vatican Pinacoteca.
26-XII-1519	On St. Stephen's Day, the tapestries are first exhibited along the walls of the Chapel under the fifteenth century frescoes.
1523	Two frescoes of the fifteenth century are destroyed by the collapse of the architrave of the entrance door.
1533	Clement VII (Giulio dei Medici) commissions Michelangelo to paint the Last Judgment on the walls above the Altar.
16-IV-1535	Paul III (Alessandro Farnese) was reigning Pope when work was begun for the fresco of the Last Judgment: frescoes of Perugino were destroyed and the wall was lined with bricks.
Summer, 1536	Michelangelo begins work on the fresco.
31-X-1541	Pope Paul III inaugurates the Last Judgment with a Vespers.
II half of XVI century	Restoration of the Sacrifice of Noah and Separation of Land and Water by Domenico Carnevali. Daniele da Volterra worked on some of the figures of the Last Judgment whose state of nudity had caused offense. Work on the two frescoes above the entrance. Enlargement of the Sacristy.
1797	The Ceiling damaged (collapse of the plaster of the Flood and of the Nude at the left of the Delphian Sibyl) by the explosion of the gun-powder works at Castel Sant'Angelo.

Study for the Last Judgment
London, British Museum

Plan of Sistine Chapel with list of paintings

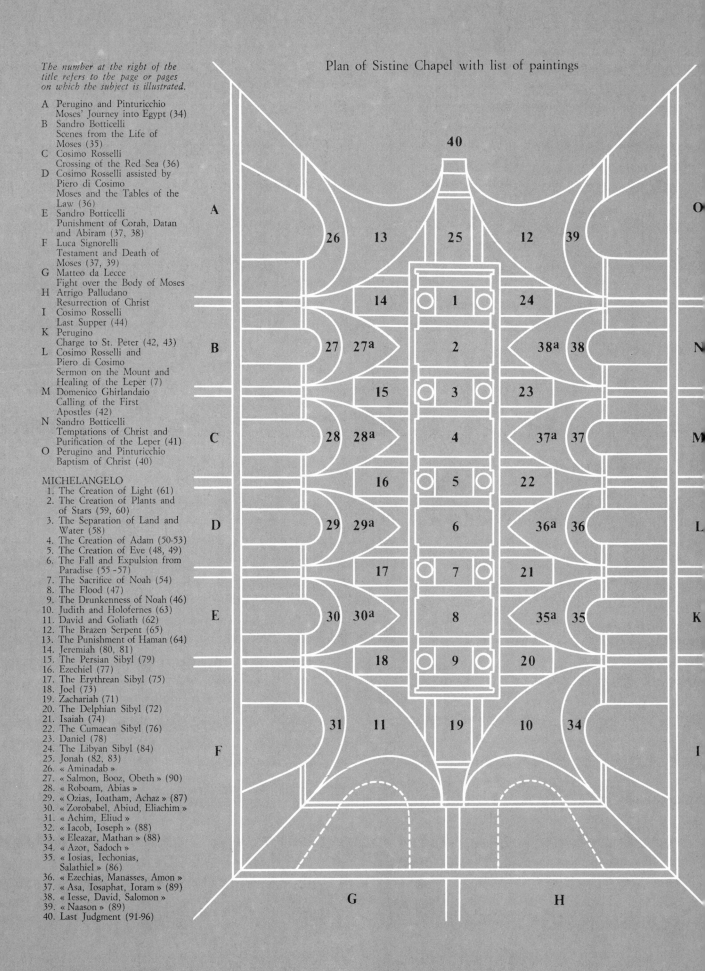

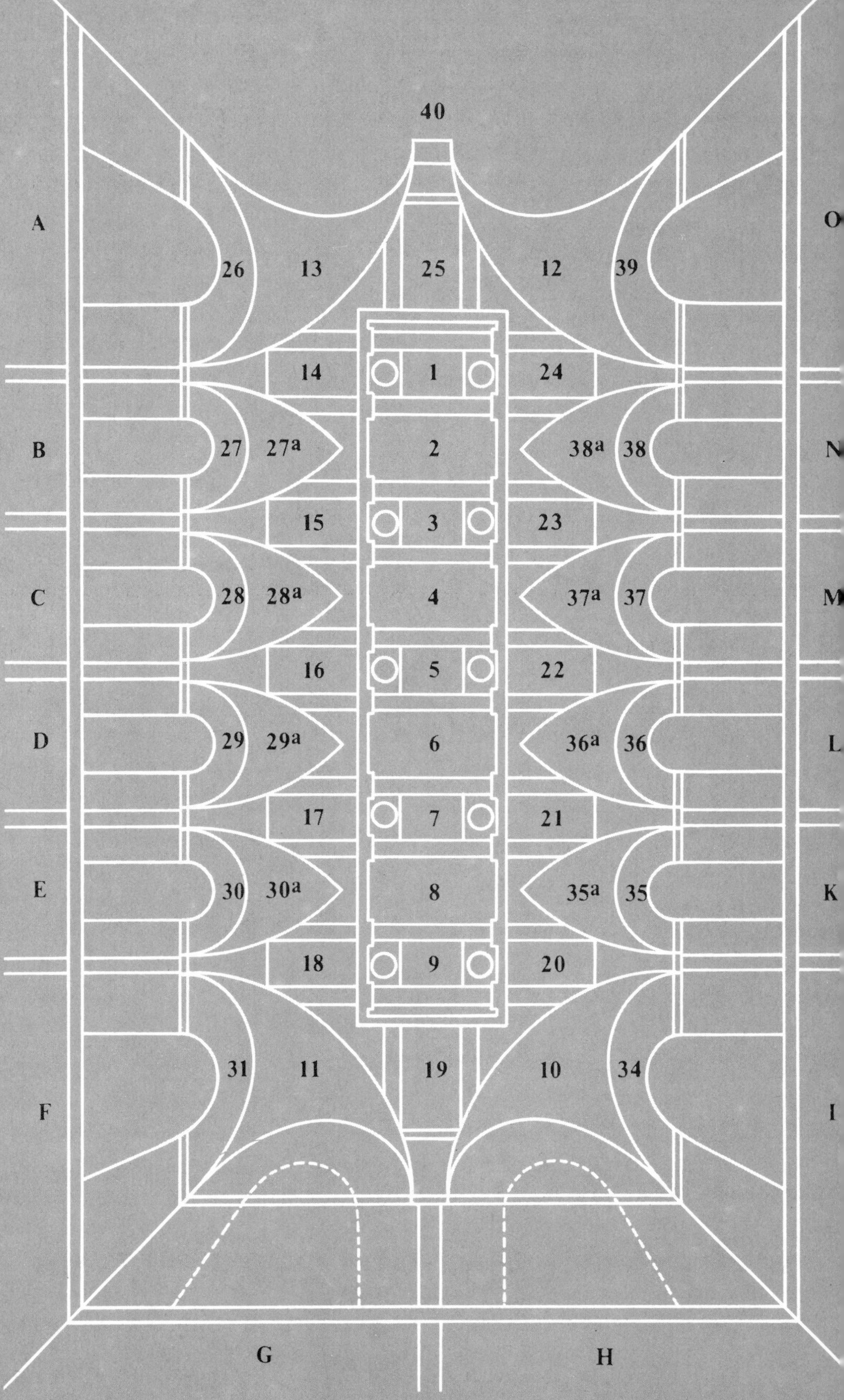

The number at the right of the title refers to the page or pages on which the subject is illustrated.

A Perugino and Pinturicchio
Moses' Journey into Egypt (34)
B Sandro Botticelli
Scenes from the Life of Moses (35)
C Cosimo Rosselli
Crossing of the Red Sea (36)
D Cosimo Rosselli assisted by Piero di Cosimo
Moses and the Tables of the Law (36)
E Sandro Botticelli
Punishment of Corah, Datan and Abiram (37, 38)
F Luca Signorelli
Testament and Death of Moses (37, 39)
G Matteo da Lecce
Fight over the Body of Moses
H Arrigo Palludano
Resurrection of Christ
I Cosimo Rosselli
Last Supper (44)
K Perugino
Charge to St. Peter (42, 43)
L Cosimo Rosselli and Piero di Cosimo
Sermon on the Mount and Healing of the Leper (7)
M Domenico Ghirlandaio
Calling of the First Apostles (42)
N Sandro Botticelli
Temptations of Christ and Purification of the Leper (41)
O Perugino and Pinturicchio
Baptism of Christ (40)

MICHELANGELO
1. The Creation of Light (61)
2. The Creation of Plants and of Stars (59, 60)
3. The Separation of Land and Water (58)
4. The Creation of Adam (50-53)
5. The Creation of Eve (48, 49)
6. The Fall and Expulsion from Paradise (55 -57)
7. The Sacrifice of Noah (54)
8. The Flood (47)
9. The Drunkenness of Noah (46)
10. Judith and Holofernes (63)
11. David and Goliath (62)
12. The Brazen Serpent (65)
13. The Punishment of Haman (64)
14. Jeremiah (80, 81)
15. The Persian Sibyl (79)
16. Ezechiel (77)
17. The Erythrean Sibyl (75)
18. Joel (73)
19. Zachariah (71)
20. The Delphian Sibyl (72)
21. Isaiah (74)
22. The Cumaean Sibyl (76)
23. Daniel (78)
24. The Libyan Sibyl (84)
25. Jonah (82, 83)
26. « Aminadab »
27. « Salmon, Booz, Obeth » (90)
28. « Roboam, Abias »
29. « Ozias, Ioatham, Achaz » (87)
30. « Zorobabel, Abiud, Eliachim »
31. « Achim, Eliud »
32. « Iacob, Ioseph » (88)
33. « Eleazar, Mathan » (88)
34. « Azor, Sadoch »
35. « Iosias, Iechonias, Salathiel » (86)
36. « Ezechias, Manasses, Amon »
37. « Asa, Iosaphat, Ioram » (89)
38. « Iesse, David, Salomon »
39. « Naason » (89)
40. Last Judgment (91-96)

PERUGINO AND
PINTURICCHIO
MOSES' JOURNEY INTO
EGYPT
detail below
left: return to Egypt
(south wall, panel I)

▷ SANDRO BOTTICELLI
SCENES FROM THE LIFE
OF MOSES
(south wall, panel II)

▷ SANDRO BOTTICELLI
SCENES FROM THE LIFE
OF MOSES
detail: daughters of Jethro

▷ SANDRO BOTTICELLI
SCENES FROM THE LIFE
OF MOSES
detail: woman helping a Jew

COSIMO ROSSELLI ▷▷
CROSSING OF THE RED SEA
(south wall, panel III)

COSIMO ROSSELLI, ▷▷
ASSISTED BY PIERO
DI COSIMO
MOSES AND THE TABLES
OF THE LAW
part below right:
Moses destroys the Tables of
the Law; adoration of the
Golden Calf; punishment of
the idolaters
(south wall, panel IV)

Side walls
Fifteenth-century frescoes
Stories of the Lives of Moses and Christ

◁ SANDRO BOTTICELLI
PUNISHMENT OF CORAH, DATAN AND ABIRAM
detail: landscape

◁◁ SANDRO BOTTICELLI
PUNISHMENT OF CORAH, DATAN AND ABIRAM
(south wall, panel V)

◁◁ LUCA SIGNORELLI
TESTAMENT AND DEATH OF MOSES
(south wall, panel VI)

LUCA SIGNORELLI
TESTAMENT AND DEATH OF MOSES
detail: death of Moses

PERUGINO AND
PINTURICCHIO
BAPTISM OF CHRIST
part below right with baptism
(north wall, panel I)

▷ SANDRO BOTTICELLI
TEMPTATIONS OF CHRIST
AND PURIFICATION OF THE
LEPER
(north wall, panel II)

▷ SANDRO BOTTICELLI
TEMPTATIONS OF CHRIST
AND PURIFICATION OF THE
LEPER
detail: woman with chickens

▷ SANDRO BOTTICELLI
TEMPTATIONS OF CHRIST
AND PURIFICATION OF THE
LEPER
detail with devil falling into
abyss

DOMENICO GHIRLANDAIO ▷▷
CALLING OF THE
FIRST APOSTLES
(north wall, panel III)

COSIMO ROSSELLI AND ▷▷
PIERO DI COSIMO
SERMON ON THE MOUNT AND
HEALING OF THE LEPER
(north wall, panel IV)

IMFNSV SALAMO
TEMPLVMTV
HOCQVARTE
SACRASTI

COSIMO ROSSELLI
LAST SUPPER
(north wall, panel VI)

◁ PERUGINO
CHARGE TO ST. PETER
(north wall, panel V)

◁ PERUGINO
CHARGE TO ST. PETER
detail: tribute money, with
Arch of Constantine

The ceiling
Michelangelo

DRUNKENNESS OF NOAH
1.55 x 2.70 ms.

◁ SISTINE CEILING
36 x 13 ms.

▷ THE FLOOD
left side

Scenes from Genesis at
the top of the ceiling

CREATION OF EVE
1.55 x 2.70 ms.

▷ CREATION OF EVE
detail of Adam

CREATION OF ADAM
detail: head of Adam

CREATION OF ADAM
detail with Eve before her
creation

▷ CREATION OF ADAM
2.80 x 5.70 ms.

SACRIFICE OF NOAH
1.55 x 2.70 ms.

▷ THE FALL
detail: Eve

▷▷ FALL AND EXPULSION
FROM PARADISE
2.80 x 5.70 ms.

SEPARATION OF LAND
FROM WATERS
1.55 x 2.70 ms.

▷ CREATION OF STARS AND
PLANTS
2.80 x 5.70 ms.

▷▷ CREATION OF STARS AND
PLANTS
detail of God

DAVID AND GOLIATH
center part
corner spandrel above entrance wall

◁ CREATION OF LIGHT
1.55 x 2.70 ms.
on the medallions
Sacrifice of Isaac
and Ascension of Elijah

▷ JUDITH AND HOLOFERNES
detail: Judith and her maid flee with the head of Holofernes
corner spandrel above entrance wall

Scenes of miraculous salvation of Israel in the four corner spandrels

BRAZEN SERPENT
center part
corner spandrel above altar wall

◁ PUNISHMENT OF HAMAN
detail with torment of Haman
corner spandrel above altar wall

▷ NUDE
above Cumaean Sibyl, right

NUDE
above Persian Sibyl, right

▷ NUDES
above Prophet Daniel
in medallion Death of Absalom

DESTRUCTION OF THE
HOUSE OF AHAB
medallion above Prophet Ezechiel

▷ PROPHET ZACHARIAH
height about 2.80 ms.

▷▷ DELPHIAN SIBYL
height about 2.80 ms.

▷▷▷ PROPHET JOEL
height about 2.80 ms.

▷▷▷▷ PROPHET ISAIAH
height about 2.80 ms.

Prophets and Sibyls around the edges of the ceiling

EZECHIEL

DANCING PUTTI
to left of Prophet Daniel

◁ PROPHET EZECHIEL
height about 2.80 ms.

◁◁ CUMAEAN SIBYL
detail

◁◁◁ ERYTHREAN SIBYL
detail

PROPHET JEREMIAH
detail: female figure at left

◁ PERSIAN SIBYL
height about 2.80 ms.

▷ PROPHET JEREMIAH
with face similar to
Michelangelo's own
height about 2.80 ms.

PROPHET JONAH
detail

◁ PROPHET JONAH
detail with whale

BRONZE NUDES
above spandrel with family
of « Roboam »

◁ LYBIAN SIBYL
height about 2.80 ms.

Ancestors of Christ in spandrels and lunettes

FAMILY OF « IOSIAS »
spandrel, height about 3.40 ms.

FAMILY OF « OZIAS »
spandrel, height about 3.40 ms

▷ « ELEAZAR - MATHAN »
lunette, about 2.15 x 4.30 ms.

▷ « IACOB - IOSEPH »
lunette, about 2.15 x 4.30 ms.

▷▷ « ASA - IOSAPHAT - IORAM »
lunette, about 2.15 x 4.30 ms.

▷▷ « NAASON »
lunette, about 2.15 x 4.30 ms.

ELEAZAR
MATHAN

IACOB
IOSEPH

ASA
IOSAPHAT
IORAM

NAASON

« SALMON - BOOZ - OBETH »
right part of lunette, with
figure probably Booz

▷ LAST JUDGMENT
13.7 x 12.2 ms.

Altar wall
Michelangelo
Last Judgment

IONAS

LAST JUDGMENT
right lunette with pillar of the flagellation carried by angels

◁ LAST JUDGMENT
detail: Virgin and Christ in Judgment

LAST JUDGMENT
detail with damned

▷ LAST JUDGMENT
detail: Charon

▷▷ LAST JUDGMENT
detail: skin of St. Bartholomew
with features of Michelangelo